**DO NOT REMOVE
CARDS FROM POCKET**

ALLEN COUNTY PUBLIC LIBRARY

FORT WAYNE, INDIANA 46802

You may return this book to any agency, branch,
or bookmobile of the Allen County Public Library.

DEMCO

THE
HEART
OF
HOLLYWOOD

THE
HEART
OF
HOLLYWOOD

A PICTORIAL HISTORY OF THE FILM CAPITAL AND
THE FAMED MOTION PICTURE AND TELEVISION FUND

BY BOB THOMAS

Designed by C. Robert Moore and Norman Noceti,
Walt Disney Studios

PRICE/STERN/SLOAN
Publishers, Inc., Los Angeles
1981

ISBN: 0-8431-0126-1

Library of Congress Catalog Card Number: 78-159751

In 1921, Hollywood was much the same as any other Southern California community, except for one thing: it was becoming known as the center of a new and unique industry.

Evidence of that industry could be seen in the picturesque Hollywood hills, where cowboys and indians chased each other regularly. And in the palm-lined streets, where comedy cops threw cream pies at fleeing robbers.

In 1921 some far-sighted Hollywood citizens, recognizing the unique nature of the new and burgeoning industry, decided that an unusual approach was needed to care for its members in times of economic trouble.

Hence the beginning of what was to become the Motion Picture and Television Fund.

The early efforts where modest. But as the need grew, the men and women of the film industry responded to the challenge.

The Fund took a giant step forward with the start, in 1932, of the payroll deduction plan. Those who could afford it were asked to donate a small percentage of their pay checks to the Fund. Payroll deductions have exceeded $2 million a year. This has continued over the years, providing the financial base for the Fund's operations.

Special gifts created the entire complex of the Motion Picture and Television Fund's Country House and Hospital. In recent years the generosity of organizations like the Screen Smart Set, the Motion Picture Mothers, and the Women of the Motion Picture Industry, along with gifts from such people as Samuel and Frances Goldwyn, Dr. Jules Stein, Lew Wasserman, George Burns, Francis Lederer, Merle Oberon Wolders, Robert Wise, Sol Lesser, Edward Small, George Seaton, Charles Feldman, The Disney Foundation, and hundreds of others – individuals and organizations–have helped to insure the future of the Fund, given spiraling costs and the ever increasing demand for the Fund's services.

During my years in the film industry, I have been pleased to observe the progress of the Motion Picture and Television Fund, and it has been my pleasure to play a role in its growth. All of us are proud of its program, which has served as a model for other industries.

This book celebrates – in pictures – the colorful history of the film community and – in words – the remarkable achievements of the Motion Picture and Television Fund.

Those achievements were made possible by the unselfish contributions in money and time by thousands of film workers, famous and unknown.

The Heart of Hollywood is dedicated to all of them.

Gregory Peck

Member of the Board of Trustees,
Motion Picture and Television Fund

Universal employees on the move west

there was nothing. Mesquite-covered hills sloping down to an arid plain. A few arroyos, dust-dry most of the year, rushing with water after the rare winter storms. Deer and coyotes came to drink. Indians shunned it as unfit to sustain life.

The Spaniards came — and went. It was a passing-through place, a way-station between the pueblo of Los Angeles and the mission settlements northward on the El Camino Real.

The first house was built of adobe by Don Tomas Urquidez in 1853.

Farmers began to arrive in the 1870s, attracted by the temperate climate. One of the early settlers was Horace H. Wilcox, from Topeka, Kansas. His wife was entranced by the new surroundings, which reminded her of the summer residence of a friend in Chicago. She gave it the same name: Hollywood.

Like all of California, Hollywood was growing. Orchards of lemons and oranges and apricots sprang up, and farmers harvested string beans and tomatoes as well as marigolds, sweet peas and other flowers.

Civic pride was growing, too. In 1903, the citizens voted 88 to 77 to incorporate as the City of Hollywood.

The new city continued to attract new inhabitants — so many, in fact, that Hollywood could not be self-sustaining. Water was badly needed for the population of 4,000, and Los Angeles was bringing water by aqueduct from the Owens River to the north. In 1910, Hollywood voted to become a part of Los Angeles.

And some curious new visitors had come to California.

✩

In late 1907, two men arrived from Chicago. One was Francis Boggs, a director for the William N. Selig motion picture company. The other was his cameraman, Thomas Persons. They made the trip to Los Angeles out of desperation.

Back at the Selig studio in Chicago, they had started a one-reel version of "The Count of Monte Cristo." Then the Illinois winter descended, and shooting could not continue.

The enterprising Boggs and Persons found a Los Angeles actor who bore a faint resemblance to their star of the Chicago version. They slapped a wig on him and finished the 12-minute film.

American audiences, fascinated by anything that moved on the nickelodeon screens, never knew the difference.

Thus encouraged, Boggs and Persons rented the roof of a

Sackett's Store and Post Office, Hollywood Blvd. at Cahuenga, 1919

downtown office building and filmed a one-reel "Carmen" in 1908; it was the first complete movie to be made in California. Colonel Selig saw the wisdom of filming under the friendly California sun, and he established a studio in the environ of Edendale, near Silverlake.

Other producers started the westward trek, and not merely for climate. The infant industry was embroiled in a battle between the Motion Picture Patents Company, which controlled the film equipment, and the independents, who declined to pay "tribute" for the use of cameras and projectors.

California afforded a comfortable distance from the detectives and lawyers of the Trust. And, if the long arm of the law did reach that far, the bootleg moviemakers could make a dash for the Mexican border.

In 1910, D. W. Griffith arrived on the first of his winter visits to California, bringing his Biograph company that included Mary Pickford, Henry Walthall, Mack Sennett, Bobby Harron and Billy Bitzer.

The first Hollywood studio was established early in 1911 by David Horsley, who leased the northeast corner of Gower Avenue and Sunset Boulevard for the Nestor Company. Hollywood afforded more space than Los Angeles, which had already become a metropolis of 500,000.

By the end of 1911, 15 film companies had settled in Hollywood

Picking sweet peas in Hollywood, 1890

Apricot orchard, Hollywood Blvd. and Cahuenga, 1900

Franklin near Bronson, 1890

Cahuenga Pass

In 1913, Cecil B. DeMille, Jesse L. Lasky, and Samuel Goldwyn rent a barn at Selma and Vine Streets to film "The Squaw Man." That was the start of a period of vast expansion of film-making in Hollywood.

D. W. Griffith returned to Califor in 1914 to film "The Birth of a Nation," which brought immediat maturity to the art of the motion picture.

Mack Sennett and his troupe of incomparable clowns set up shop the Keystone Studio in Edendale. Carl Laemmle established Univers in Hollywood, then moved to a big site in the San Fernando valley. Lasky bought a ranch near

Vitagraph settled in East Hollywood. Triangle built a big studio in Culver City. William Fox created a studio on Sunset Boulevard.

By 1917, the Motion Picture Trust had been defeated, but film makers continued the rush to California. Mary Pickford and Charlie Chaplin announced plans to base their operations in Hollywood. Louis B. Mayer, Thomas Ince and William S. Hart were among those who established new production companies.

The film community was taking form. Although studios were located from Edendale to Culver City and movie workers lived in all parts of Los Angeles, Beverly Hills and other cities, the universal name for the film colony became — Hollywood.

Like all communities, Hollywood was beginning to develop a conscience.
In the early years, it had been like a gold rush town. People came and went, not knowing when the world's fascination with films might end.

Now it appeared that movies were no passing fancy, but were indeed developing into a full-scale industry. With that status came social and civic responsibilities.

The 1917-18 war brought changes.

Highland Ave. north of Hollywood Blvd., 1906

Beverly Hills Hotel, 1913

Nestor Studio, Sunset and Gower

Vitagraph Studio

Hollywood realized its ability to play an important role in the national emergency. The studios turned out patriotic films to bolster morale. Stars like Mary Pickford, Douglas Fairbanks, Charlie Chaplin and Marie Dressler helped sell Liberty Bonds. Others participated in recruiting and in entertaining doughboys at army camps.

And, for the first time, the film industry realized the need for taking care of its own. Many film workers who had been drafted or who had enlisted left families behind. The beginnings of Hollywood's concern for its own citizens came with efforts to raise money for the support of the families of servicemen.

In 1918, 2000 movie workers, ranging from the most famous stars and directors to prop men and extras, gathered in William Clune's Auditorium in downtown Los Angeles. Mary Pickford, D. W. Griffith and others cited the need to care for the wives and dependents of film workers who had gone to war.

Jesse L. Lasky views his first studio, 1913

Universal Studio

First Selig Studio in Edendale

Selig Studio

The Halperin Company. Among the performers: Tiny Ward, Dot Farley, Creighton Hale, Dale Fuller, Stuart Holmes, Zasu Pitts, Polly Moran, Snitz Edwards, Sid D'Albrook, Thomas Meighan

Fifty thousand dollars in pledges was raised by the meeting. The Motion Picture War Service Association administered the funds.

The armistice brought new problems to Hollywood.

Studios found themselves stuck with backlogs of movies about the war, and the public now wanted to forget the war. The influenza epidemic swept through the country, and doctors advised people to stay away from theaters and other public places.

The movie industry was jolted, and many of the studios shut down. Hundreds of workers lost their jobs. Some went back to the theater or vaudeville, but most could find no other income. The charitable efforts which had been devoted to servicemen's families were now directed toward destitute workers. But there was no organization; funds were generally raised by passing the hat.

Obviously a better solution had to be found.

Keystone studio banquet at Levy's Cafe, 1915. L-R, top row: Mrs. Mack Swain, Mrs. Chester Conklin, Dorothy Davenport, Miss Wallace, Mack Swain, Teddy Sampson, Ford Sterling, Charlie Murray, Ad Kessel, Mrs. Charlie Murray. Second Row: Chester Conklin, Lottie Pickford, Minta Durfee, Roscoe Arbuckle, Mabel Normand, Mack Sennett. Front Row: A. L. Ries, Mother Davenport, Phyllis Allen, Harry "Mother" McCoy, Mrs. Syd Chaplin, Syd Chaplin

Selig stars and featured players; glass stage in background

A benefit affair during World War I — William S. Hart (upper left); D. W. Griffith (middle left); Carlyle Blackwell (lower left); Charlie Chaplin and Douglas Fairbanks (upper right); Roscoe Arbuckle (middle right); Douglas Fairbanks, Donald Crisp and Rudolph Valentino (lower right)

Warner Studio announces the advent of sound

brought a period of consolidation to Hollywood. The influenza epidemic had passed, and so had the film industry depression. The postwar boom that accompanied the nation's return to normalcy created an enormous appetite for the entertainment that movies could provide. The nickelodeon toy had become big business.

Wall Street was quick to recognize the potential profits in films.

Small companies were merged into big corporations, and their stocks were sold to the public. Loew, Pathe, Fox, Metro-Goldwyn-Mayer and Universal were traded on the New York Stock Exchange. A group of independent film makers formed First National. Mary Pickford, Charlie Chaplin, Douglas Fairbanks and D. W. Griffith were too high-priced to be hired by any company, and so they created United Artists.

It was an extravagant time.

Theaters resembling mosques and tabernacles rose in the major cities of America. Lavish entertainments were needed to fill such temples, and movies grew more and more expensive. Spectacles like "Ben-Hur," "The Ten Commandments" and "The Covered Wagon" added new dimensions to the screen.

Most of the film companies maintained their head offices in New York, but Hollywood had become the production capital. Studios were growing, and salaries for top talent became astronomical. Hollywood was everyone's dream as a place to get rich in a hurry.

Inevitably, there were those whom success eluded, and the unfortunate of Hollywood became a matter of increasing concern.

The Motion Picture War Service Association had continued welfare activities for returning veterans and their families but something more was needed. Leaders of the Association met at the Griffith studio and discussed a new organization that would broaden its scope to offer help to all needy workers in the industry.

Frank Woods, chief supervisor of Famous Players-Lasky, was designated to organize such a group. But the plan encountered opposition from the Actor's Fund of America, which feared conflict with its own charitable activities. The idea of a movie charity was dropped.

In 1921, the film industry organized a benefit pageant at the Beverly Hills Speedway, which raised $20,000 for the Actor's Fund. Broadway producer Daniel Frohman, president of the Fund, came to Hollywood to supervise the benefit, and industry leaders suggested establishing a west coast branch to help film workers. Frohman agreed.

Hotel Hollywood

Beverly Hills, 1926

The Motion Picture Branch of the Actor's Fund held its first meeting in the tea room of the Garden Court apartments on August 4, 1921.

George Woods presided as chairman. Mark Larkin, publicity chief for Mary Pickford, served as secretary, and W. J. Reynolds as treasurer. Committee members included actress Winifred Kingston, actor Mitchell Lewis, writers Marion Fairfax and Mary O'Connor, and Will Wyatt, manager of the Mason Opera House and official representative of the Actor's Fund.

On September 22, 1921, the committee held its second meeting

Annual Horse Show Parade on Rodeo Drive, 1925

and Treasurer Reynolds announced receipt of $1000 from Frohman to establish an Emergency Fund for charity work in the motion picture industry. The need for an administrator was discussed. Rev. Neal Dodd was suggested as the best possible candidate.

Rev. Dodd was a remarkable man. At a time when many of the nation's clerics were assailing Hollywood as a citadel of sin, he became one of the town's staunchest defenders. An Episcopal priest, he had established his first Hollywood church in a vacant store in 1918. Not only did he welcome movie

Hollywood Bowl, 1922

Bridal shower for Gloria Swanson. L-R, Yvonne Skelton, Claire Windsor, Marion Davies, Gloria Swanson, Constance Talmadge, Adela Rogers St. Johns, Louella Parsons

Mary Pickford, her cast and crew, at her birthday party

people as parishioners; he became one of them. In his lifetime he portrayed ministers in more than 300 films.

On September 29, 1921, Rev. Dodd reported to the committee the first disbursement of assistance: $40 to pay the hotel bill and rent an apartment for an acting couple.

The husband had been a character actor for 37 years and his wife had been in the chorus. Both had appeared in movies for eight years. Now he was partially paralyzed and unable to work. Besides providing for lodging, Rev. Dodd arranged with Lasky's and Realart for the wife to be called for work.

The second case was a widow who was living in a tent with her four children. Lasky's studio provided lumber and carpenters to make the tent livable for the winter, and casting offices were asked to supply acting jobs for the woman.

Mrs. Cecil B. DeMille and committee for the Studio Club building campaign

Douglas Fairbanks with advertising for Don Q

As more cases came to the committee's attention, additional funds were needed. The first in a long series of star-packed benefits was held in Clune's Auditorium in 1923.

Donald Crisp organized the program, which included most of the important stars in Hollywood. Mary Pickford appeared in a skit. Will Rogers did his roping act, and Charlie Chaplin performed a pantomime. A suit of armor appeared to be a stage prop; toward the end of the show

Exploitation for The Kid

Grauman's Egyptian Theater

Million Dollar Theater

Playing cards at Paramount: L-R around table, Robert Castle, Jean Arthur, Lane Chandler, Clara Bow, Bebe Daniels, Doris Hill, Neil Hamilton

it moved and the audience was startled to discover that Douglas Fairbanks was inside.

Soon it had become apparent that motion picture charity could no longer be administered as an adjunct of the New York-based Actor's Fund. The affiliation was dissolved. The Motion Picture Relief Fund of America was incorporated under the laws of the state of California, December 31,19

Joseph M. Schenck became the first president. Mary Pickford, a

Wampas Baby Stars at the pool: L-R, Mrs. Reginald Denny, Helen Ferguson, Mrs. Jean Hersholt, Ruth Roland, Laura LaPlante, Ruth Clifford

Walt Disney and his cartoon staff

Sennett comedians: L-R, Ralph Graves, Vernon Dent, Andy Clyde, Billy Bevan, Dot Farley, Eugenia Gilbert, Alice Day, Sid Smith, Thelma Hill

Plan of Chaplin studio

Chaplin Studio on La Brea Ave.
during freak snow storm

Educational Studio

Hal Roach Studio

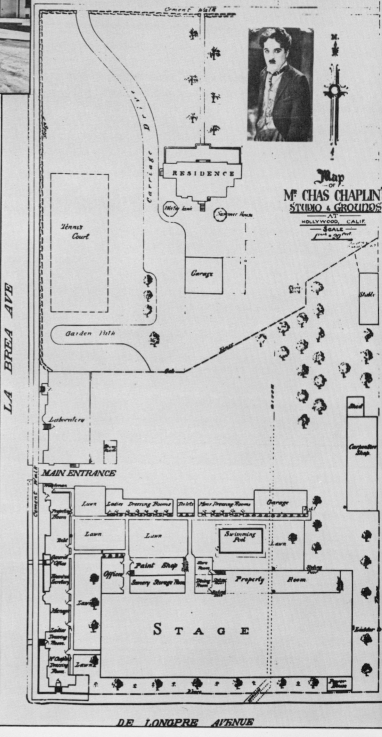

Fox Studio, Western Avenue

guiding force in the organization since its beginnings, was named vice president. Rev. Neal Dodd continued to administer the case investigations.

The first Board of Trustees of the Relief Fund included Harold Lloyd, Douglas Fairbanks, Mae Murray, William S. Hart, Cecil B. DeMille, Jesse L. Lasky, Charles Christie, Robert Fairbanks, Donald Crisp, Frank Woods, Fred Beetson, Hal Roach, Rupert Hughes, Rob Wagner, Ewell D. Moore, Irving Thalberg, Wedgewood Nowell and Alfred A. Cohn.

The Fund continued to grow.

Mr. and Mrs. Harold Lloyd, Marion Davies, Sid Grauman at an industry dinner

In the first year of operation as part of the Actor's Fund, $700 had been disbursed to 18 persons. By 1924, 125 recipients had been given $22,000.

In the beginning, Rev. Dodd had operated from his own church office. In 1923 he hired the Fund's first employee, a stenographer. The following year the first social worker was employed.

Rudolph Valentino, William S. Hart, Douglas Fairbanks, Norma Talmadge, Joseph Schenck at the Los Angeles depot

Will Rogers welcomed as Mayor of Beverly Hills, 1926

The Twenties brought almost unrelieved prosperity to Hollywood. A new era was signalled on October 6, 1927, when Warner Brothers premiered "The Jazz Singer," the first feature film with dialogue and synchronized music.

Sound created an industrial convulsion. But by the end of the decade the nation's theaters had converted to sound, and they were prospering as never before. In 1929, 110,000,000 tickets were sold each week, nearly double the amount for silent films two years before.

Not even the Stock Market Crash of October 29, 1929, could diminish the public's fascination with talkies. Americans seemed to need entertainment more than ever, as a means of escaping their humdrum lives.

Talkies created hundreds of new careers — and destroyed others. Many actors, directors and writers were deemed unfit for the new medium. Most of them had not foreseen the end of their golden times, and they failed to provide for their futures.

The Motion Picture Relief Fund came to the aid of such persons

A charity affair in the 1920s. Among those visible: Marion Davies, Charles Chaplin, D. W. Griffith, Mary Pickford, Harry Crocker, Mayor James Walker of New York, Polly Moran, Anita Stewart, Adolphe Menjou, Adela Rogers St. Johns, Jimmy Shields, Gloria Swanson

Samuel Goldwyn and Henry King on the set of The Winning of Barbara Worth

The Our Girls Club, 1926. L-R, back row: Juliane Johnstone, Zasu Pitts, Billie Dove, Ruth Roland, Claire Windsor, Gertrude Olmstead, Carmel Myers, Carmelita Geraghty, Helen Ferguson, Patsy Ruth Miller, Lois Wilson. Front row: Virginia Valli, Laura LaPlante, Gloria Hope, Virginia Fox, Mary Pickford, Pauline Garon, Mildred Davis, May McAvoy, Clara Horton, Edna Murphy

Henry de la Falaise, Colleen Moore, Hedda Hopper, Frank Barham, Frances Goldwyn, Buddy Rogers, Lawrence Gray, Phyllis Haver, Ruth Taylor, Constance Talmadge, Blanche Sweet, Buster Collier, Ed Hatrick, Claire Windsor, Howard Hughes

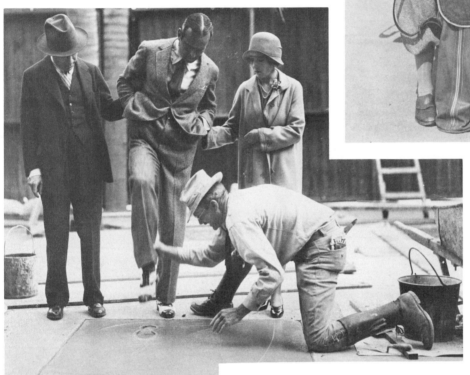

Douglas Fairbanks, Jr. and Sr.

Douglas Fairbanks and Mary
Pickford with Sid Grauman,
the cement ceremony at
Grauman's Chinese

Douglas Fairbanks, Will Hays
and Mary Pickford entertain
former President and Mrs.
Calvin Coolidge

and others whose luck had gone bad. Among the case histories:

William H. (Daddy) Taylor, 102 years old, a Confederate veteran and a bit player for 17 years. Relief Fund workers convinced him to enter a sanitarium when he grew too feeble to keep house for himself.

Mary Carr, who starred as the mother in "Over the Hill" and "Paying the Price," was sued for three months' back rent by her landlord. The Relief Fund represented her in court and found a new home for her.

Joseph H. Hazelton, 76 and ill, was supported by the Relief Fund. He had been a program boy at Ford's Theater the night President Lincoln was shot. When he sold an account of the tragedy to a magazine for $50, he sent the check to the Fund, saying, "I want to be a life member."

The uniqueness of the Motion Picture Relief Fund was apparent from the beginning. An early account in "Hollywood Magazine" reported:

"Red tape has been carefully and conscientiously avoided . . . there is none, which puts the Fund in a class by itself. Promptness is another moving factor . . . the speed with which aid is given is often times of more importance than the aid itself. 'Relief first and questions afterward,' might be the motto of the Fund — for that is how it works."

Douglas Fairbanks, Mary Pickford, Charles Lindbergh, Marion Davies, Louis B. Mayer

A luncheon for Winston Churchill at MGM: William Randolph Hearst, Churchill, Louis B. Mayer, Fred Niblo, John Churchill

White Mayfair Ball at the
Victor Hugo: Anita Louise,
Janet Gaynor, Gene Raymond,
Marion Davies, Dolores Del Rio

brought the big-studio era to Hollywood. The new dimension of sound had added sophistication to the screen, and the demand for movie entertainment was enormous.

The studios geared to accommodate that demand. Contract players were signed by the hundreds, and each studio employed long lists of producers, directors, writers and technicians on a year-round basis. Such staffs were needed to turn out a movie a week, as most of the big studios were doing.

The movie boom sometimes faltered. In 1933, with sound no longer a novelty and the nation in the depths of the Depression, 5000 of the country's 16,000 movie houses were shuttered. Studio staffs were trimmed, and those remaining on salary were asked to take cuts of 50 per cent. Two of the companies faced receivership.

As the nation's economy improved, so did the film business.

A brilliant new galaxy of stars added glamor to the screen. Directors and writers explored fresh areas of social comment. Theater owners provided the added incentive of Bank Night and free dishes to lure customers.

The Motion Picture Relief Fund strove to keep up with the added welfare demands of an expanded industry.

The Fund attracted the support of the industry's greatest leaders. Following Joseph M. Schenck as president were Cecil B. DeMille, Carl Laemmle, Mary Pickford, Jack L. Warner, Jesse Lasky, Conrad Nagel and Marion Davies.

THE 30's

Money raising remained haphazard. A charity ball. A benefit premiere. A polo match. Fashion shows and card parties.

Such events brought new finances to the Motion Picture Relief Fund. But they weren't enough to keep ahead of the need.

In 1932, the Fund dispensed $190,000 to needy film workers, but only $155,000 was received in donations. The remaining $35,000 had to be borrowed, and an appeal for money was made to high-salaried film workers.

A better system of financing was imperative.

Carole Lombard's cocktail party at the Brown Derby Bamboo Room: Robert Taylor, Irene Hervey, Carole Lombard, Cesar Romero

Posing in the penny arcade: 1) *Billie Dove;* 2) *Mildred Davis Lloyd;* 3) *Marie Mosquini;* 4) *Unidentified;* 5) *Bebe Daniels;* 6) *Polly Mason Gallagher;* 7) *Unidentified;* 8) *Howard Hughes;* 9) *Ben Lyon;* 10) *Harold Lloyd;* 11) *Roy Brooks;* 12) *Hoot Gibson* 13) *Skeets Gallagher*

The payroll deduction plan for those earning over $200 a week was instituted in 1932. Studio workers were asked to earmark one-half of one per cent of their earnings to the Motion Picture Relief Fund. The response was good, and the Fund was able to accommodate the needs of a thousand film workers whose luck had gone sour.

During the early Thirties, the Fund occupied an office over the Bank of America at Santa Monica Blvd. and Western Ave. Then in 1934, the headquarters was moved to 5444 Hollywood Blvd., near Central Casting.

Father Neal Dodd remained as executive secretary, and Anne Lehr, wife of studio executive Abraham Lehr, served as director on a volunteer basis. There were 10 paid employees, but much of the work was done by volunteers.

Such figures as Mrs. Samuel Goldwyn, Mrs. Tod Browning, Charlotte Greenwood, Mrs. Antonio Moreno, Mrs. Sam Wood, Mrs. Richard Wallace and Mrs. Conrad Nagel spent hours in the Fund office interviewing applicants.

Five social workers made the allocations. They were given a certain amount each day — about $200 if the Fund was solvent — to dispense on cases.

The year 1938 was a fateful one for the Motion Picture Relief Fund.

The Fund was reorganized to provide a broader base of

Night club scene. L-R: Maurice Chevalier, Gloria Swanson, Irving Thalberg, Norma Shearer, Herbert Marshall

A 1936 party for Daniel Frohman (seated). L-R: Mrs. D. W. Griffith, Allan Jones, Irene Hervey, Robert Montgomery, Mary Pickford, Errol Flynn, Una Merkel

Turf Club Ball at the Ambassador Hotel. L-R: Charles Boyer, Virginia Bruce, Tyrone Power, Loretta Young, Pat Paterson, David Niven, Mrs. Henry Fonda, Henry Fonda

participation. The administration was now conducted by the talent groups, unions and producer representatives. The funding situation was greatly improved by the Screen Actor's Guild ruling for compulsory contributions by its Class A members of one-half of one per cent of their salaries.

Also in 1938, Jean Hersholt came home one night from a Relief Fund board meeting at Jack Warner's house.

"You're going to think I'm crazy," he told his wife, "but they talked me into being President."

text continued on page 42

Douglas Fairbanks and Harold Lloyd entertain visiting Japanese Navy officers

MGM luncheon for Secretary of the Navy Swanson. L-R: Marion Davies, Wallace Beery, Unidentified, William Randolph Hearst, Swanson, Louis B. Mayer, Will Rogers

MGM visit by Edsel Ford and family. Child actors in foreground: Mickey Rooney, Cora Sue Collins (fourth from left), Freddie Bartholomew, Jackie Cooper

Reception for Italian Ambassador Rosso, given by Louis B. Mayer. Stars, L-R: Jeanette MacDonald, Helen Hayes, Nelson Eddy, May Robson, Jean Harlow, Constance Bennett, Maureen O'Sullivan

Walt Disney with Lionel, Ethel and John Barrymore

The Stars: Janet Gaynor, Shirley Temple, Will Rogers, Conchita Montenegro, John Boles, Rochelle Hudson, Victor McLaglen, Peggy Fears, Lew Ayres, Rosemary Ames, Edmund Lowe, "Pat" Paterson, James Dunn, Helen Twelvetrees, Stepin Fetchit, Henry B. Walthall, Gilbert Roland, Herbert Mundin, Norman Foster, Claire Trevor, Spencer Tracy, Alice Faye, Warner Baxter, Ketti Gallian

It was a brilliant choice. Born in Copenhagen, Jean Hersholt had come to Hollywood in 1913 and soon established himself as one of the most distinguished of character actors. He sometimes played villains, but he was more convincing in the kindly roles that were closer to his nature.

Hersholt had accepted presidency of the Relief Fund only after the producers promised to wipe out the deficit. That was done, and then he searched for a way to supplement the income from payroll deductions.

The opportunity came in 1939 with the premiere of a new radio program, ''The Screen Guild Show.''

Jules Stein of MCA provided the impetus for the show. The idea was to have top stars of the movies appear on the weekly broadcast, donating their normal

Broadcasting from the Warner Brothers radio station, KFWB. L-R: Patricia Ellis, Joe E. Brown, Lloyd Bacon, Jack Warner, Edward G. Robinson, Mervyn Leroy, Bebe Daniels, Ken Murray, Paul Muni (in costume for I am a Fugitive from a Chain Gang), *Glenda Farrell, David Manners*

Stan Laurel, Walt Disney, Oliver Hardy

A gathering of Warner Brothers contract actresses. Standing, L-R: Evalyn Knapp, Lila Lee, Winnie Lightner, Joan Blondell, Claudia Dell. Sitting: Marian Marsh, Louise Fazenda, Unidentified, Ona Munson, Irene Del Roy, Laura Lee, Marian Nixon, Loretta Young

salaries to the Motion Picture Relief Fund. Members of the Directors and Writers Guilds also contributed their services to the program.

Gulf Oil agreed to sponsor the series, and "The Screen Guild Show" made its premiere over 61 CBS stations on January 8, 1939.

The first program starred Jack Benny, Judy Garland, Joan Crawford and Reginald Gardiner in a musical revue based on an idea by Morrie Ryskind and directed by Mitchell Leisen.

"The Screen Guild Show" quickly became one of the most popular programs on network radio. Studios permitted condensed versions of their films, and the casts were always high-powered.

Every star agreed to donate one performance per year, and some played more often. Ralph Morgan, president of the Screen Actors Guild and a devoted worker for the Fund, once thanked Charles Laughton for appearing on the show.

"Thank me?" said Laughton. "I'm thanking you. It's every actor's duty."

The Fund was receiving $10,000 a week from the show, and the money was placed in reserve for a particular dream of Jean Hersholt's — a permanent residence and hospital where the motion picture industry could take care of its own.

During 1939, reported Treasurer George Bagnall, the case load jumped 63 per cent from 410 to 642 families, representing

Founding members of the Screen Actors Guild: L-R, seated: Alan Mowbray, Lucille Gleason, Boris Karloff, Ralph Morgan, Noel Madison. Standing: Kenneth Thomson, Jimmy Gleason, Ivan Simpson, Richard Tucker, Clay Clement, Claude King, Alden Gay Thomson, Bradley Page, Morgan Wallace, Arthur Vinton

A quartet of distinguished directors: Frank Lloyd, Henry King, John Ford, Frank Borzage

Costume party. Louella Parsons, William Randolph Hearst, Sr. and Jr., Marion Davies

Posing at a party: Jack Oakie, Ginger Rogers, John Gilbert

Fredric March with Mary Brian at his birthday party

At the premiere of A Midsummer Night's Dream: *Jack Warner, Max Reinhardt, William Randolph Hearst*

Carl Laemmle with visiting Albert Einstein

15,825 individuals. Expenditures had climbed to $279,000.

A typical month's cases:

    Unemployment aid — 261
    Emergency aid — 23
    Medical care — 277
    Dental care — 21
    Major operations — 7
    Patients in hospitals — 48
    Rest home cases — 8
    Sanitarium cases — 4
    Funerals — 2
    Medical appliances — 10
    Special nurses — 9

Case workers also handled situations which were unique to the movie industry. An indigent actor required a toupee to get film work. A young actress needed to have her teeth capped. An alcoholic writer required a drying out before he could be employed. A dress extra had to get his tuxedo out of hock.

"We don't ask a lot of questions," said Mary Pickford, who had

text continued on page 49

Backstage at a benefit. L-R, seated: Madeleine Carroll, Samuel Goldwyn, Clark Gable, Carole Lombard, Shirley Temple, Myrna Lo
Tyrone Power. Standing: Ralph Morgan, Melvyn Douglas, Charles Laughton, Reginald Owen

Stars at a benefit: Maurice Chevalier
and Jeanette MacDonald

Playing pool at Arline Judge's cocktail party: Jack Oakie, Edward G. Robinson,
Clark Gable, Arline Judge, Carl Brisson

Assistance League Skating party. L-R: Toby Wing, Tom Brown, Shirley Ross, Cesar Romero, Cora Sue Collins, Mary Carlisle, Henry Fonda

Polo at the Riviera Club. Robert Montgomery, Jack Holt

Poolside gathering: Jeanette MacDonald, Dolores Del Rio, Norma Shearer, Ernst Lubitsch

Watermelon eaters at Screen Boys Club meeting: Freddie Bartholomew, Mickey Rooney, Jackie Cooper

Spencer Tracy, Walt Disney, Jimmy Gleason, Frank Bor

been named President Emeritus because of her long devotion to the Fund.

"We see the need and we fill it. Pride means a great deal to people in our business."

Hollywood finished the decade with a burst of creativity.

David O. Selznick produced the magnificent "Gone with the Wind." The Civil War epic dominated the 1939 Academy awards with 10 Oscars, but there were other classic films that year as well: "Stagecoach," "The Wizard of Oz," "Goodbye, Mr. Chips," "Wuthering Heights," "Ninotchka," "Mr. Smith Goes to Washington," "Of Mice and Men," "Love Affair," "Dark Victory," "Juarez."

The film business was prospering as never before. Even the beginning of war in Europe failed to dim the optimism over Hollywood's future.

Hattie McDaniel receives her supporting actress Oscar for Gone with the Wind *from Fay Bainter*

Maurice Chevalier gets some pointers from William S. Hart

Dating at the premiere of Captains Courageous: *Mickey Rooney and Judy Garland*

THE FORTIES . . .

brought war — and new conflicts to Hollywood.

The war between Nazi Germany and the Franco-British Alliance was felt in Hollywood more than in most American communities. David Niven, Laurence Olivier and other members of the British colony had left to join the English forces.

Hollywood had portrayed the nature of the Nazi menace in such films as "The Mortal Storm," "Escape," "Confessions of a Nazi Spy" and "Four Sons." The film community was active in raising funds for such causes as Greek War Relief, United China Relief, Bundles for Britain and Russian War Relief.

When the United States entered the war on December 7, 1941, Hollywood's involvement became total.

Twenty-nine thousand movie workers entered the Armed Forces during World War II, including scores of the world's most famous names. The Hollywood Victory Committee was formed to book stars to entertain in veteran's hospitals and army and navy bases all over the world.

Hal Roach and Walt Disney studios were converted to the production of training and morale films. John Ford, George Stevens, William Wyler, John Huston and other top notch directors headed units of cameramen in the battle zones.

Star caravans toured the major cities to sell Victory Bonds. At home, Bette Davis organized the Hollywood Canteen, where stars entertained and washed dishes for visiting servicemen.

The film industry had been shaken by the loss of its overseas market; virtually all of Europe and much of Asia were closed to American movies.

But the wartime demand for entertainment offset the foreign losses.

The Forties

SWINGING ON A STAR

ars of the Hollywood Victory Caravan received by Mrs. Franklin D. Roosevelt at the White House. L-R, seated: Oliver Hardy, Joan
ondell, Charlotte Greenwood, Charles Boyer, Risé Stevens, Desi Arnaz, Frank McHugh, Matt Brooks, James Cagney, Pat O'Brien,
nidentified, Alma Carroll. Standing: Allan Scott, Merle Oberon, Eleanor Powell, Arlene Whelan, Marie McDonald, Faye McKenzie
ehind hat), Kathryn Booth, Mrs. Roosevelt, Frances Gifford, Frances Langford, Elyse Knox, Cary Grant, Claudette Colbert, Bob
ope, Ray Middleton, Joan Bennett, Bert Lahr, Jack Rose, Unidentified, Stan Laurel, Jerry Colonna, Groucho Marx

Junkets in the early 1940s. South Bend premiere for Knute Rockne, All American. *Standing, L-R: Irene Rich, Ricardo Cortez, Bob Hope, Gail Patrick, Anita Louise, Franklin D. Roosevelt, Jr., Mrs. Bonnie Rockne, Jane Wyman, Pat O'Brien, Gale Page, Rosemary Lane, Rudy Vallee. Front row: Charles Ruggles, Owen Davis, Jr., Jimmy Fidler, Donald Crisp, Ronald Reagan*

The Dodge City junket. Standing, L-R: Rosemary Lane, Gilbert Roland, Frank McHugh, Maxie Rosenbloom, Priscilla Lane, Errol Flynn, John Garfield, Unidentified, Wayne Morris, Unidentified, John Payne, Alan Hale. Front row: Unidentified, Hoot Gibson, Ann Sheridan, Buck Jones, Guinn "Big Boy" Williams, Humphrey Bogart, Jean Parker, William "Hopalong Cassidy" Boyd

Servicemen on leaves jammed big-city theaters. War workers sought the diversion of a movie after their shifts, and many theaters operated 24 hours a day to accommodate them.

Movie theater admission in the United States totaled $735,000,000 in 1940. By 1942, the figure had passed a billion; by 1945, it was $1,450,000,000.

The Motion Picture Relief Fund continued its growth.

Studio employment was high, and payroll deductions supported the welfare program. Meanwhile the building fund received the steady income from "The Screen Guild Show." During the program's lifetime, it contributed $5,300,000 to the Fund.

After the total had passed the half-million mark, Jean Hersholt decided it was time to make the move.

One day he and his wife Via were driving through the San Fernando Valley when he decided to call at a real estate firm called Bob's Good Earth. Hersholt had previously bought property there for the Danish Old People's Home, and he inquired if any other large lots were available.

"Yes, there's a 48-acre spread in Woodland Hills that may be available," he was told. "There has been a death in the family, and they might sell."

The Hersholts looked at the acreage, which was planted in walnuts and oranges.

Former Earl Carroll comics at the ground breaking for Carroll's Theater Restaurant: Jack Benny, W. C. Fields, Cantor, with announcer Bill Goodwin

Party Scene: Frank Borzage, Spencer Tracy, Hedy Lamarr, Robert Taylor

"That's it," said Hersholt, and he wrote out his personal check as a down payment.

He brought the Relief Fund Board of Directors to Woodland Hills and presented the proposal. Some of the board members were dubious, considering the site too distant from Hollywood.

"If you don't want it, I'll buy it," said President Hersholt.

The Board agreed to buy. The price: $850 per acre.

On September 22, 1941, leaders of the motion picture industry gathered at the former John Show ranch to break ground for the first buildings of the Motion Picture Country House.

Mary Pickford and Jean Hersholt turned the first shovelfuls of earth.

Presidents of the major associations and guilds made speech of support: Y. Frank Freeman for the producers, Edward Arnold for the actors, George Stevens for the directors, Sheridan Gibney for the writers.

The Santa Fe Trail *junket to Santa Fe, N.M. Standing, L-R: May Robson, William Orr, Errol Flynn, Allan Jones, Martha O'Driscoll, William Lundigan, Wanda McKay, Nancy Carroll, Natalie Draper. Front row: George Tobias, Suzanne Carnahan (Susan Peters), Rita Hayworth, Brenda Marshall, Reginald Gardiner*

Cast for The Screen Guild Players: *Bing Crosby, Bob Hope, Betty Grable, Kay Kyser, Howard Duff. Foregound: Harry Ackerman*

The Screen Guild Players: *Edward Arnold, Barbara Stanwyck, Gary Cooper, Harry Ackerman*

The Virginia City *junket: L-R on horseback: Priscilla Lane, Ronald Reagan, Unidentified, Brenda Marshall, Rosemary Lane, Errol Flynn, William Boyd, Wayne Morris.*

Donald Crisp presents James Stewart with his Oscar at the Academy awards

Architect William Pereira told a reporter of his plan:

"In the center of these rolling acres will be our small city composed of bungalow residences and various types of community-use separate buildings. The library, lounge, dining room, administration buildings and outdoor recreation facilities are arranged on terraces overlooking two lagoons. Everything is connected by broad roads, covered walkways and interesting footpaths."

The outbreak of war three months later made completion of the first buildings difficult. But a year after the ground breaking, the place was ready to be occupied.

On the day before the dedication, Jean Hersholt was talking with Louis B. Mayer.

"You must be very proud, Jean," said Mayer. "Is there anything I can do to help?"

Film figures in uniform at the
Academy awards: Ronald Reagan and Jane Wyman

ger Rogers and James Stewart

Darryl F. Zanuck and Norma Shearer

n Hersholt presents Humphrey Bogart with scroll
oring actors who had appeared for The Screen
ld Players radio show

Brenda Marshall and
William Holden

Hollywood Bond Cavalcade in New Orleans. L-R, seated: Mickey Rooney, Judy Garland, Lucille Ball, Rosemary LaPlanche, Unidentified, Muriel Goodspeed, Harry Babbitt. Standing: Kay Kyser, Dick Powell, Georgia Carroll, Fred Astaire, Greer Garson, James Cagney, Ish Kabibble

"Yes, you can give the dining room." Mayer agreed to do so.

On September 27, 1942, three thousand members of the film community gathered in Woodland Hills for the dedication of the Motion Picture Country House.

"This project," said California's Governor Culbert L. Olson, "is evidence of the unselfish hearts of the people of the motion picture industry, who at all times come forward to give their talents and services in time of need."

The first buildings included bungalows to house 24 residents; the Sidney R. Kent Memorial Clinic with 18 beds; the Y. Frank Freeman library; lounge, dining room and administrative office.

With the Country House a reality, the Motion Picture Relief Fund continued its welfare activities in the community.

Jane Wyman entertains at Fort Logan, Denver

Betty Grable eats chow at the Bakers and Cooks school, Fort Jackson, N.C.

Ann Sheridan greeted by soldiers on a USO tour

Ingrid Bergman dines with GIs on camp tour

The war boom helped ease the case load; many unemployed film workers found employment in aircraft plants and other war industries. But many others were unable to support themselves, and the Relief Fund came to their aid.

The headquarters had moved to a new location on Santa Monica Blvd. at Mansfield Ave. Wilma Bashor, who had come to the Fund as a vacation relief worker in 1931, now served as executive director.

Rehearsing for the Bond Cavalcade: Jose Iturbi, Lucille Ball, Harpo Marx, Fred Astaire

Jam session aboard Hollywood Victory Caravan. Players: Joan Blondell, Cary Grant, Marie McDonald, Groucho Marx, Bert Lahr. Listeners include Frances Langford, Irving Newman, Charles Feldman, Alfred Newman, Johnny Maschio and Joan Bennett

Close harmony on Hollywood Victory Caravan. L-R, seated: James Cagney, Charlotte Greenwood, Groucho Marx. Standing: Cary Grant, Faye McKenzie, Stan Laurel, Frances Langford, Pat O'Brien, Risé Stevens, Frank McHugh

Joe E. Brown entertains at the Hollywood Canteen with Jimmy Dorsey

Onstage for the Hollywood Bond Cavalcade: James Cagney

In 1942, the Fund dispensed $450,000 for 7,422 cases, and most of that amount came from payroll deductions. The surplus reflected the accrued income from the radio show: $1,350,000, compared to $125,000 in 1938.

The growing surplus brought closer another dream: the Motion Picture Country Hospital. But that had to wait until the end of the war.

The ground-breaking took place on July 7, 1946.

On April 18, 1948, the Motion Picture Country Hospital was dedicated. It provided complete medical facilities, including 40 private rooms and 10 surgical beds. The cost: $1,350,000.

The film industry was enjoying the postwar boom, and employment was high. The Relief Fund received strong support from the payroll deduction plan and from community efforts as well.

But by the end of the 1940s there were signs of trouble in the film economy.

The industry was affected by changing times. The government had forced studios to divorce themselves from their theater chains. Affluence was spreading, and the public was seeking new diversions.

The Motion Picture Relief Fund was hard hit. To offset the loss of revenue, the Friars Club staged an all-star extravaganza in 1949 which raised more than $300,000 for the Fund.

Most of all, television presented a threat to the movies' hold on the American public. That threat was to be realized in the 1950s.

Irene Dunne christens the Liberty Ship USS Carole Lombard *as Clark Gable, Louis B. Mayer and Mrs. Walter Lang observe*

Duet for the Bond Cavalcade: Judy Garland, Mickey Rooney

Bob Hope presents a replica of a movie star stamp book, which was sold to benefit the Motion Picture Relief Fund, to Princess Margaret as Queen Elizabeth, King George VI and King Michael of Rumania look on

Command Performance: Jimmy Durante, Ginny Simms, Nelson Eddy, Fred Allen

Kathryn Grayson in Chicago War Bond Parade

Command Performance: Ingrid Bergman, Bing Crosby

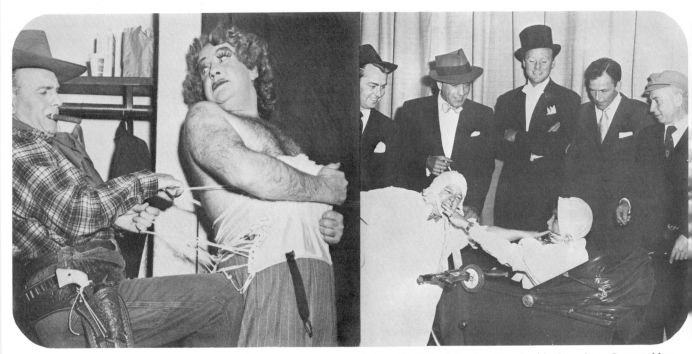

George Burns helps Broderick Crawford into his costume

Baby skit, Friars' Frolic: Alan Ladd, Humphrey Bogart, Van Johnson, Frank Sinatra, Harpo Marx and midgets

Ensemble fo
Friars' Fr
Foreground: (
Kelly. L-R,
Peter Law
Ray Mil
Walter Pidg
Fred MacMu
Van Johr
James Ste
Robert Ta

Dedication of the Motion Picture Country Hospital. L-R before cameras: Y. Frank Freeman, Jean Hersholt, Robert Young, Shirley Temple, Ronald Reagan, Mayor Fletcher Bowron of Los Angeles

Ground-breaking for the Motion Picture Country Hospital. L-R: William Pereira the architect, Loretta Young, Jean Hersholt, Mary Pickford, Edward Arnold

THE FIFTIES . . .

brought the full force of television into competition with the motion picture industry. Television had grown from gross revenue of $1,900,000 in 1947 to $106,000,000 in 1950. By 1958, the figure had passed a billion dollars.

Millions of Americans sat transfixed as they watched the antics of Milton Berle, the clowning of Lucille Ball, the exploits of Hopalong Cassidy.

The film business suffered from the loss of audiences. Business was off 20 to 40 per cent.

Theater receipts began a decline from the all-time high of $1,692,000,000 in 1946. By 1958, the total had fallen to $992,000,000.

Hollywood used its ingenuity to survive.

A technological revolution had saved the industry in the 1920s; new ways were sought to lure customers back to the theaters: Cinerama, CinemaScope, Todd-AO, VistaVision, 3-D.

The new dimensions helped, but the American public remained fascinated by the free entertainment on the home screen.

The old order was changing.

Economy-minded studios could no longer afford the long lists of contract players, directors and writers. Studio workers in all categories were laid off or retired.

Film companies realized they could neither ignore nor combat television. They began releasing their backlogs of feature films for home viewing. They also entered the field of producing television series.

The Fifties

Academy winners, 1956: Dorothy Malone, Anthony Quinn, presenter Anna Magnani, Yul Brynner, Buddy Adler, Cary Grant (accepting for Ingrid Bergman)

Winners Grace Kelly and Marlon Brando at Academy awards

Television employment helped pick up the slack in film employment. But the work volume was not the same. To many film workers, the 1950s brought financial distress.

The Motion Picture Relief Fund was ready to help.

In 1951, the headquarters moved to modern facilities at 335 N. La Brea Ave., where the increased case load could be accommodated. The new building provided 8000 square feet of floor space, affording room for a clinic. Previously, case workers had to refer patients to local hospitals or clinics.

The radio show, now called "The Screen Guild Players," continued until 1952, having added a steady $10,000 a week to the Relief Fund.

Oscar rehearsal: Clark Gable, Cary Grant, Bob Hope, David Niven

An attempt was made to convert the show to television after the decline of network radio. The effort failed. The loss of income meant that the Relief Fund would have to rely primarily on contributions from members of the industry. Their support continued to be strong.

At the 1952 annual meeting, Executive Secretary Wilma Bashor reported that the Fund had been able to assist 7188 film workers and their families during the previous year.

President Emeritus Mary Pickford told the meeting:

"It is incredible to realize the great work that has been done by the Fund. I am so proud when I go out to the Country House and Hospital.

Shirley Booth on television screen as she accepts her Oscar in New York

Walt Disney shows Disneyland to his grandson

Opening day at Disneyland

"Some of us remember when film people were dying in rooming houses, all alone and with strangers.

"It is a long time since I made a picture, but one day on a set an extra came to me and thanked me for the help she had received from the Fund.

"She said she was taken ill in the middle of the night. Her husband called the Fund President, and without any red tape, an ambulance was sent. She was taken to a hospital and operated on; her life was saved.

"I feel very proud to be part of an organization such as the Motion Picture Relief Fund."

At the Khrushchev luncheon: Bob
Hope, Mrs. Khrushchev, Frank Sinatra

Nikita Khrushchev views Juliet
Prowse and other Can-Can dancers
at 20th Century-Fox. Also in the
party: Henry Cabot Lodge, Eric
Johnston, Spyros Skouras, Anita
Louise, Mrs. Khrushchev

Other guests at the
Khrushchev luncheon:
George Cukor, Marilyn
Monroe, Clifton Webb

First-nighting at the
Cocoanut Grove: Elizabeth
Taylor, Michael Wilding,
Judy Garland

Studio conversation: John
Wayne, Humphrey Bogart,
Lauren Bacall

Jerry Lewis clowns during set visit of Russia's Anastas I. Mikoyan and son

In 1955, a 21-bed Country Rest Home was opened. Staffed by a resident physician and a crew of nurses, it provided much-needed space for recuperating patients from the Country Hospital.

On May 17, 1956, the industry's leaders gathered at the Beverly Hills Hotel for a banquet honoring Jean Hersholt's humanitarian service.

He told the audience:

"When I came to this country 44 years ago, I had $20 in my pocket. The good heart of the picture industry was immediately opened to a virtual stranger when I hadn't the money to pay for hospitalization.

Golf benefit in Palm Springs. Dean Martin, Harpo, Groucho and Gummo Marx, Bing Crosby and starlets

Stars at a golf benefit: Bob Hope, Jerry Lewis, Dean Martin

Mary Pickford visits President and Mrs. Eisenhower to kick off 1953 Teasury Bond Drive

Top: *Oldtimers reunion at Pickfair: Antonio Moreno, Mary Pickford, Jack Mulhall, Buster Keaton, Charles Rosher (behind camera)*
Left: *Harold Lloyd with Charles Ruggles;* Right: *Buster Keaton, William Boyd, Zasu Pitts, Grace Bradley Boyd*

'This was the basis for my interest in people who needed help.

'You have made for me the most memorable evening of my life.''

He had left a hospital bed to attend the banquet and the next day he returned. Two weeks later he succumbed to cancer.

Samuel Goldwyn learning a dance step from Roland Petit at a set party of Hans Christian Anderson

Jack Warner strolls through his studio with Field Marshall Montgomery

Benay Venuta, Errol Flynn and Jack Benny in Korea

Bob Hope in Korea

Press Photographers Ball: Cesar Romero
and Joan Crawford

Judy Garland and Donald O'Connor

George Bagnall, who had served as director, treasurer and
vice president, was elected to succeed Jean Hersholt
as president of the Motion Picture Relief Fund.

With the film economy unstable and more film workers
reaching retirement, additional facilities were
needed at the Motion Picture Country House and Hospital.

Construction began in 1959 for a $350,000 addition which
would provide hospital and sanitarium space for
0 beds. The new facility brought the total
investment to $2,500,000.

Ann Blyth and
Roddy McDowell

Changes in the film business continued at an astonishing rate.

Louis B. Mayer left the studio that bore his name.
Harry Cohn, founder and absolute ruler of Columbia, was claimed by death. Darryl F. Zanuck relinquished control of production at 20th Century-Fox.

Gone was the era when a handful of studio bosses controlled the destiny of the film business.

Independent producers were on the ascendant. Stars and agents wielded new power.

By the end of the decade, television sets in the United States had multiplied 10 times to 50,000,000.

The film industry felt the impact. Twenty-five per cent of the nation's theaters had closed their doors forever. During the decade, production of features by major companies had dropped from 320 to 189 per year.

Vera-Ellen and Rock Hudson

Frank Sinatra with Frank Jr. and Nancy at Academy awards, 1952

Another hazard had been added to menace Hollywood's well-being: overseas production.

Government subsidies, cheap labor, tax benefits and the advantage of exotic scenery had lured one-third of American film-making to Europe.

The American film industry was struggling for its life. But it had always been a good fighter.

Writers Guild awards banquet: Merle Oberon, Ronald Reagan

Directors Guild awards: George Stevens, Darryl F. Zanuck, George Marshall, Fred Zinnemann, Joseph L. Mankiewicz

Screen Producers Guild tribute to Cecil B. DeMille. L-R, front row: Jesse Lasky, Virginia Grey, Loretta Young, Julia Faye, Walter Brennan, Jane Darwell, Unidentified, DeMille, Barbara Stanwyck, Reginald Denny, Kathlyn Williams, Claudette Colbert, Raymond Hatton, Susan Hayward, Katherine DeMille, Beu

di, Eddie Quillan. Back row: Rod LaRoque, Fredric March, Ben Alexander, Richard Cromwell, Ricardo tez, Paul Kelly, Yul Brynner, Laraine Day, Charlton Heston, William Boyd, Lon Chaney, Gary Cooper, d Bond, Anthony Quinn, Herbert Wilcoxon, James Stewart

THE SIXTIES . . .

proved another decade of trial for the film industry. The
decade began with strikes by actors and writers.
Their actions appeared to demonstrate the concern of all
film workers over the future of the movie business.

Their fears seemed well grounded.

After sliding throughout the 1950s, film theater admissions
leveled off at $900,000,000 during most of the 1960s,
nearly a 50 per cent drop from the 1947 high.
Meanwhile the nation's population had risen by 40 million.

The corporate structure began to change.

MCA dissolved its giant talent agency and took over
Universal. Darryl Zanuck returned to 20th Century-Fox and
revived its failing fortunes.

Wall Street renewed its interest in movies despite the
industry's troubles. Giant corporations were searching for
investments to cash in on the growing leisure time of
the American public. Film companies seemed a natural.

Academy awards, 1968, Los Angeles Music Center

the SIXTIES

Emmy Awards, 1963. Charles Boyer and David Niven accept award for their late partner, Dick Powell

Emmy Awards, 1962. Onstage: Lucille Ball, Carl Reiner, Bob Newhart

Dedication of Samuel Goldwyn Plaza: L-R: George Bagnall, Jules Stein, Lucille Ball, Mr. and Mrs. Goldwyn, Jack Warner

Dedication of the Samuel Warner Wing. Walter Pidgeon, Donald Crisp, Jack Warner, Jane Wymar

United Artists was merged with Transamerica. Paramount wa
bought up by Gulf and Western. Warner Brothers was
sold to Seven Arts, later to Kinney National Service. Embass
was taken over by Avco.

There seemed to be good reason to believe that the film business would prosper. The television networks had discovered
the drawing power of Hollywood features, and movies playe

every night in prime time. The selling price for features to television soared.

Most of all, the industry realized that profits from topflight attractions could prove almost limitless.

Of the 25 all-time moneymaking films, 19 were released in the 1960s, including the astounding ''The Sound of Music,'' first movie to attract more than $100,000,000 in rentals.

The Motion Picture Relief Fund entered its fifth decade with confidence.

In 1961, members of the industry met in Woodland Hills once again to dedicate an addition to the Country House and Hospital. This time it was The Pavilion, an 80-bed facility for recuperative patients.

In 1961, Wilma Bashor resigned as executive director after 30 years of devoted service to the Fund. The Board searched for a successor and found one in William T. Kirk, who had been with the International Social Service agency in New York.

Dedication of the John Ford Chapel: George Bagnall, Virginia Grey, Ford, William Kirk

Elvis Presley presents donation to Relief Fund: Chester Conklin, Frank Sinatra, Presley, George Bagnall

In the face of a changing industry, the Relief Fund could not stand still. A Development Committee, headed by George Seaton, was formed to study future needs.

The Development Committee discovered some hard facts.

The average age of film workers in 1944 was 44. Twenty years later it was 54 and climbing.

The Woodland Hills plant was 20 years old. Parts of it, especially the hospital, were in need of modernization.

Fund raising faced a crisis. With studio staffs cut down, the payroll deduction plan could not fulfill all future needs. New means of financing were essential.

Another discovery of the survey was the fact that supplying entertainment for television had become a principal function of the motion picture industry. The inter-dependence of the two mediums made the title of the Motion Picture Relief Fund obsolete. The new name of the organization became: The Motion Picture and Television Relief Fund.

Douglas Fairbanks, Jr. with bust of his father at Country House

Dedication of the Louis B. Mayer Theater:
Walter Pidgeon, Greer Garson, Debbie Reynolds,
George Murphy, Edward G. Robinson,
George Bagnall

Louis B. Mayer
1885 - 1957

In October of 1964, a major new program was announced.

The immediate plans: a $600,000 expansion of the Hospital, adding a 60-bed wing for long-term care patients; the Louis B. Mayer Memorial, including a theater, chapel and facilities for occupational and recreational therapy; addition of service facilities, including staff quarters, laboratory, clinic, pharmacy and central kitchen.

A large order. But a bigger plan was also involved: a 15-year development program.

The Endowment and Building Campaign needed a special kind of chairman, a man widely known and respected in the community.

Theater Owners of America 1965 Star of the Year winner, Julie Andrews, with former winners Gregory Peck, Jerry Lewis, James Stewart, John Wayne

Charlton Heston in the cement at Grauman's Chinese

Viewing plans for Country House expansion: Gregory Peck, George Bagnall, Rock Hudson, Roy Disney

Dick Van Dyke learning technique from Stan Laurel

Golden Globe Awards: John Wayne and Ann-Margret

Gregory Peck had long been acquainted with the Motion Picture and Television Relief Fund and was among its staunchest supporters. He was asked if he would head the drive. "Certainly," he replied.

The growth of the Relief Fund was demonstrated by the 1964 figures. Costs of the Woodland Hills plant were $1,476,297. The Hollywood headquarters disbursed $850,337. The record total: $2,326,634. The Fund had assisted 8,118 individuals.

Response to the Endowment and Building Campaign was strong.

Samuel Goldwyn donated $250,000 to create the Samuel Goldwyn Plaza, 16 double cottages with recreational areas. The Disney Foundation gave $250,000, bringing its total to $500,000. The Hollywood Canteen Foundation: $100,000. Jack and Ann Warner gave $300,000 to build the Samuel Warner Wing.

Lloyd Haynes and Patty Duke

Henry Gibson, Carol Burnett, Julie Sommars

Dinner for King Olav of Norway: King Olav, Jack Valenti, Mr. and Mrs. Greg Morris

A hundred thousand came from a television Salute to Stan Laurel starring Dick Van Dyke. Benefit premieres of ''The Great Race'' and ''My Fair Lady'' added to the total.

The Country House and Hospital were benefiting from other bequests as well:

The Laemmle Wing, memorializing Carl Laemmle and Rosabelle Laemmle Bergerman, a gift of Stanley Bergerman.

The chapel, donated by John Ford.

Ford also donated real estate and other bequests which brought his total to more than a quarter-million. James R. Webb also contributed real estate. Donations of $50,000 came from Lew Wasserman, George Seaton, the Robert Wise Foundation, Elvis Presley, and the estate of Jean and Don Harvey.

Gregory Peck gave $75,000. A hundred thousand was given by Bob Hope and another $100,000 by Jules and Doris Stein. Lori Bara willed $222,000 in the memory of Theda Bara.

An added windfall was the sale of a 12-acre parcel of land for a shopping center adjacent to the Country House and Hospital. It had been purchased for $19,000 in 1941. The selling price in 1964: $1,100,000.

Bequests from estates also contributed to the total. Among those who willed large sums to the Fund: Elizabeth Risdon, Albert Lewin, Clifton Webb, Charles Feldman.

Feldman had made a habit in his lifetime of donating several thousand dollars to the Fund each Christmas in the name of his talent agency clients. His will left more than $3,000,000 to the Fund.

King Olav and Jack Valenti with Edward G. Robinson and James Stewart

Fellow Campaigners: Bob Hope, John Wayne, Ronald Reagan, Dean Martin, Frank Sinatra

Donations have come in many forms and amounts, from the Feldman bequest of millions to $25 left by a grateful secretary. The gifts have been in the form of cash, securities, property, memorials, term trusts, bequests, gifts subject to life income, payroll deductions and insurance. All, except for payroll deductions, were used to expand the facilities of the Motion Picture Country House and Hospital, to build the endowment fund or to establish memorials.

Despite the increasing case load, social workers continued to treat each case with sympathy and understanding. And the unique nature of the movie breed was always considered.

Dinner for Lord Mountbatten: Cary Grant, Dyan Cannon, Lord Mountbatten, Y. Frank Freeman

Reception at Universal Studio: Princess Margaret, Frank McCarthy, Walt Disney, Jules Stein

Princess Margaret and Lord Snowden watch the stunt-man show at Universal with Mr. and Mrs. Jules Stein

A one-time star lived in a big home and owned an expensive car but had no money to buy groceries. His obligations were paid and he was convinced to live more modestly until a break came along.

A top director had overplayed his hand financially and was about to lose his house. A check for $5,000 helped tide him over.

A writer lost all ambition after his wife died. He sold his belongings until there was nothing to sell. A hometown friend offered him a newspaper job in the middle west. The Fund bought him a new wardrobe and plane fare.

Celebrity race for benefit of the Motion Picture and Television Relief Fund at Ontario Motor Speedway: James Garner

Paul Newman and Mario Andretti

Academy awards, 1960. Peter Ustinov, Shirley Jones, Elizabeth Taylor, Burt Lancaster

Academy awards, 1969: Cary Grant, Frank Sinatra

Academy awards, 1969: Fred Astaire

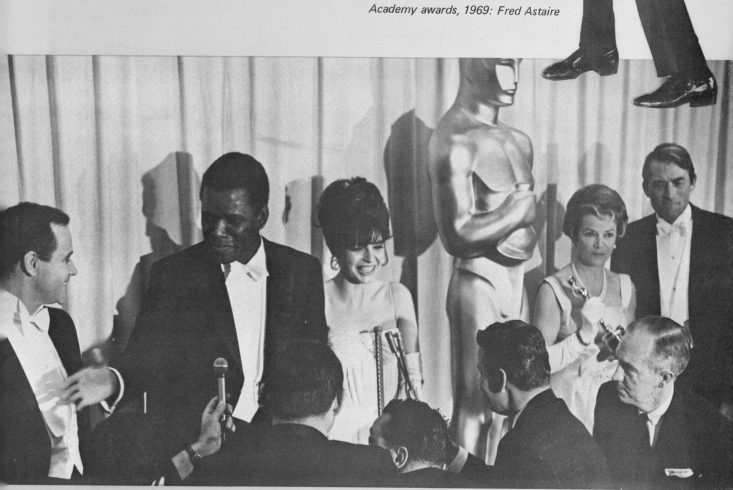

Academy awards, 1963: Jack Lemmon, Sidney Poitier, Anne Bancroft, Annabella, Gregory Peck

Stars gather for a group portrait at Paramount:
Yves Montand and Barbra Streisand

A character actress's sole asset, a $7500 diamond brooch, was in hock with interest due. The Fund redeemed it, sold it, took back its money, and gave the rest to the actress.

No notes or loans are ever required in such cases. The recipient is told: "If you get back on your feet, you can give the money back." Many do make the repayment.

The end of the Sixties brought wholesale change.

Censorship restraints had been cast off, and the new films brought frankness — and criticism — to the film medium.

A series of expensive failures had shaken several of the movie companies with huge losses.

Economic uncertainty caused vast unemployment in Hollywood, spreading hardship through every guild and union.

Henry Hathaway, Lee Marvin, Rock Hudson, Clint Eastwood

John Wayne, Kim Darby

The Portrait: Lee Marvin, Rock Hudson, John Wayne, Yves Montand, Clint Eastwood, Barbra Streisand

But, as always, there was hope.

Films such as "The Graduate," "Bonnie and Clyde," "The Love Bug," "Funny Girl," "True Grit," "Midnight Cowboy," "Easy Rider," "Butch Cassidy and the Sundance Kid," "Airport," "Patton," "M*A*S*H" and "Love Story" proved that the audience was unlimited for the right attraction.

A whole new generation had embraced film as its mode of expression. The young crowd flocked to see the movies that interested them.

And a new and exciting generation of film makers was rising to fulfill that need.

Entertaining in Vietnam: Phyllis Diller and Bob Hope

Bob Hope and Raquel Welch in Vietnam

Oscar winner of 1964, Julie Andrews, with ~~Sidney Poitier~~ Sidney Poitier

98

Reception at the Ambassador Hotel: Robert Taylor, Ursula Theiss, Anna Maria Alberghetti, Nancy Reagan, Rosanno Brazzi, Ronald Reagan

Hollywood in the 60s

Bust of Jean Hersholt
at Country House

The Seventies...

Entrance to Motion Picture Country Hospital

MOTION PICTURE HOSPIT

THE SEVENTIES . . .

heralded the 50th anniversary of the Motion Picture and Television Relief Fund's unique achievement in welfare.

On June 13, 1971, the greatest entertainers in the show world appeared at the Los Angeles Music Center in an extravaganza to commemorate the Fund's half-century.

Another anniversary observance was a program of symposiums and conferences concerning the medical aspects of the Fund.

George Bagnall, William Kirk and Gregory Peck discuss the future as they stroll the Country House grounds

"No other industry provides such a welfare plan that is supported by both labor and management," said Bill Kirk.

"No other industry offers such a wide variety of care."

The gradations of care available to those who qualify:

1. Acute hospital treatment — skilled personnel and the most modern of facilities.
2. Extended care — for convalescent and chronic cases.
3. Outpatient care, both medical and dental.
4. Protected residential facilities — guest bungalows with all needs supplied.
5. Apartment residential facilities — a future plan to house retired workers.
6. General Social Service — helping persons in time of need.

Tram transports guests to nearby shopping center

Barbara Hale, George Kennedy, Lloyd Nolan, George Seaton, William Kirk and Bill Williams attend one of the movies screened three times a week at the theater

Dennis Day, Betty Gelman, Social Service
Director, and Jack Staggs, Associate
Executive Director for the Fund

John Ford Chapel

Country House grounds

103

Milton Berle, Peter Graves, Jack Benny and Steve Allen appear at the Country House to plan a benefit premiere

Entrance to Louis B. Mayer theater

Dining Room, Country House

An impressive program, especially in view of the fact that a potential of 94,000 persons would be eligible for such care.

The size of the program could be seen in the Relief Fund's 1970 budget: $4,173,482. Now 433 persons were employed, compared to 50 in the early 1960s.

The future?

"If we can raise 40 million," said President George Bagnall, "the future will be secure."

"So far we have never borrowed a dime for building, and we don't intend to. We've never had a year in the red since the Country House opened. Good times or bad, we've never sacrificed services."

Donald Crisp, Anna Lee and Walter Pidgeon attend a barbecue before screening in the Mayer theater

Physical therapy for hospital patients

Art class for Country House guests

Frank Sinatra and Rosalind Russell with plaque commemorating fifty years of service to the Hollywood community by the Motion Picture and Television Relief Fund.

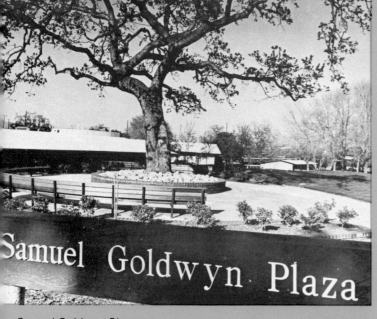

Samuel Goldwyn Plaza

On July 27, 1971, the Board of Trustees arrived at a momentous decision. In keeping with the philosophy of the Fund and the services it provided to the members of the industry, the word "Relief" was eliminated. It then became The Motion Picture and Television Fund.

Aerial view of the Motion Picture Country House and Hospital

The library at the Country House

Looking ahead...

In the decade since this book was published, the Motion Picture and Television Fund has moved steadily toward the fulfillment of its initial dream. Under the dedicated leadership of George Bagnall, the Fund, with grace and wisdom, has provided services for the urgent needs of thousands of industry members. The Fund is grateful that voluntary payroll deductions and special gifts enabled it to provide the essential maintenance of its buildings and grounds and have made possible the refurbishing of the Country House and Hospital.

Now, there is another dream, a dream of expansion. Sloping gently to the south of the Country House and Hospital are some twenty lovely acres. It is this land which ultimately can be developed into additional retirement residences and medical facilities so vital to the future. It is here that the Fund can look forward to the continuance of its visionary program, a program to provide care and attention in an atmosphere of dignity and love. A committee headed by Fund President Jack Dales and Executive Director Jack Staggs is now developing a master plan for extension and expansion which will carry the Country House and Hospital into the 21st century.

Royalties from the sale of this book are donated to the Motion Picture and Television Fund.

Acknowledgement

The author is grateful to many persons for their assistance in research for this book. Mary Pickford, Jack L. Warner, Sol Lesser, Mrs. Jean Hersholt, William T. Kirk, George Bagnall, Harry Ackerman, George Seaton, Wanda Tuchok and Florence Homan were especially generous with their time and memories.

preparation. Through the courtesy of Card Walker, services and talent were donated. C. Robert Moore and Norman Noceti designed the book, and Tom Jones and Gabe Essoe were helpful in locating photographs.

Finding the photographs proved a major project. They came from both private and public sources, and many persons helped in the search. Among them: Mrs. Samuel Goldwyn, Howard Strickling, Duke Wales, Bernie Williams, Dr. Robert Knudson, Ray Stuart, Gene Lester, Ken Murray, Frank Purcell, Buck Harris, Albert M. Thompson, Matty Kemp, Chuck Panama, Madison Lacey, Ernest E. Sloman, Mildred Simpson, Mort Likter, Bob Goodfried, Victor Plukas, Clarence Inman, Bill Shaeffer, Bill Faith.

A note about the captions. Unfortunately, many of the photographs bore no caption, and many of the identities had to be guessed at or omitted.

Photo Credits Key

Albert B. Rosenfelder Collection: pages 14, 25, 29. *Ambassador Hotel:* pages 72, 89, 99. *A&M Records:* page 28. *Academy of Motion Picture Arts and Sciences:* pages 26, 31, 33, 43, 49, 56, 57, 67, 68, 69, 78, 94, 99. *Academy of Television Arts and Sciences:* page 83. *Association of Motion Picture and Television Producers:* pages 58, 59, 60, 61, 62, 63, 64, 73, 76, 91, 92, 98.

Bob Hope: pages 74, 76, 98. *Beverly Hills Chamber of Commerce:* pages 20, 21.

Directors Guild of America: page 79. *Friars Club:* page 64. *Gene Lester:* pages 27, 51, 53, 55, 60, 61, 63, 68, 70, 73, 77, 78, 87, 88.

Harry Ackerman: page 55. *Hollywood Chamber of Commerce:* page 99. *Hollywood Museum:* pages 12, 13, 15, 20, 21, 24, 26, 27, 28, 32, 36, 38, 45, 49, 53, 72. *Harshe-Rotman & Druck:* pages 95, 96. *Huntley Services:* page 91.

Jim Eddy Associates: pages 94, 95. *Jack L. Warner:* pages 45, 76. *Ken Murray:* pages 16, 17, 22, 23, 29, 30, 31, 42, 44.

Los Angeles County Museum: pages 8, 9, 32. *Louis B. Mayer Foundation:* pages 33, 39, 40. *Larry Edmunds Book Shop:* page 18.

Martin Kearns: pages 24, 25, 28, 32. *Madison Lacey:* pages 28, 42. *Mary Pickford:* pages 74, 75. *Motion Picture and Television Relief Fund:* pages 57, 63, 65, 84, 85, 86, 88, 100-107.

Paramount Pictures Corporation: pages 96, 97. *Producers Guild of America:* pages 80, 81, 99. *Ray Stuart:* pages 34, 36, 37, 38, 44, 46, 47, 48, 49, 61, 87.

Screen Actors Guild: page 43. *Samuel Goldwyn:* pages 31, 46, 48, 75. *Security Pacific National Bank:* pages 8, 9, 10, 11, 12, 13, 23, 30.

Twentieth Century-Fox: pages 41, 71, 72.

Warner Brothers: pages 52, 54. *Walt Disney Productions:* pages 27, 40, 42, 48, 70. *William Gleeson:* page 22. *Writers Guild of America:* page 79.

Universal Studio: pages 9, 93. *University of Southern California:* pages 14, 15.

Firooz Zahedi page 5

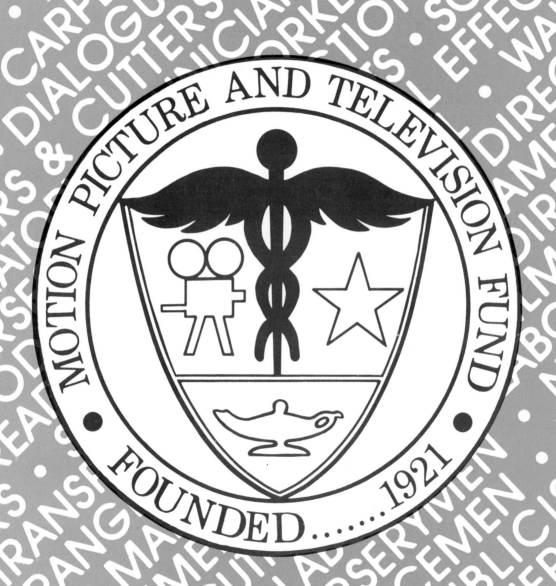

MOTION PICTURE AND TELEVISION FUND

FOUNDED 1921